The Super 30-Day Home Cleaning Plan

Making Time to Beat the Grime

Judith Turnbridge

© 2014 Judith Turnbridge

Disclaimer and Terms of Use: The Author and Publisher has strived to be as accurate and complete as possible in the creation of this book, notwithstanding the fact that he does not warrant or represent at any time that the contents within are accurate due to the rapidly changing nature of the Internet. While all attempts have been made to verify information provided in this publication, the Author and Publisher assumes no responsibility for errors, omissions, or contrary interpretation of the subject matter herein. Any perceived slights of specific persons, peoples, or organizations are unintentional. In practical advice books, like anything else in life, there are no guarantees of income made. This book is not intended for use as a source of legal, business, accounting or financial advice. All readers are advised to seek services of competent professionals in legal, business, accounting, and finance field.

First Printing, 2014

Printed in the United States of America

Table of Contents

About This Book

There are plenty of cleaning schedules out there, and a bewildering number of websites on the topic, so why bother buying this book in the first place? That's a good question, and hopefully this opening chapter will provide you with a definitive answer! My book offers far more than just another monotonous cleaning schedule. In fact, it tackles the hardest part of housework: motivating yourself to do it in the first place!

I should know – I totally HATED housework – totally, utterly hated it! Then I grew up, got married, and had kids. So, over the years I have had no choice but to come up with a number of strategies for dealing with it. Now, I actually *enjoy* doing housework (well, most of the time, anyway). I take great pride in feeling that I'm providing a clean, tidy, and safe environment for my family to live in and that I'm able to keep on top of things. I also get a great sense of achievement because I've conquered my aversion to cleaning. (I bet my mom would never have thought that when I was living at home!)

Most surprisingly, I've discovered that housework can be truly therapeutic! There's something about the act of cleaning that, once you accept you have to do it, is actually relaxing (well for me anyway).

"But, wait a minute," – I hear you cry – "why do it yourself in the first place? Can't I just get someone to do the work for me, like a maid or a cleaning service?"

Yes, that's certainly an option. But, unless you're going to employ someone around the clock to clean up after you, then you will still have to do some of it yourself at one time or another. When you factor in the high cost of employing a cleaning service, the lack of privacy (do you really want someone you hardly know to be rummaging through your underwear drawer?), and worrying about your employee's honesty, then it begins to look like a pretty unattractive proposition. (Can you really be sure your housekeepers would not be tempted to help themselves to your groceries, an odd little trinket, or maybe even your precious jewelry?)

Moreover, by getting someone else to do your cleaning, you'll never be able to experience that wonderful sense of pride and achievement that you'll feel when you've actually done the chores yourself.

There's one other thing to consider. Although its health benefits appear to have been overstated recently in the press, (and by some of the less competent health agencies) housecleaning is still a great way to promote flexibility in your body, as it forces you to stretch and bend as you work.

So, now that I've introduced this book (and hopefully convinced you that doing your own housework is a good thing), let's begin by taking a look at the key to domestic Nirvana: the cleaning schedule!

Introducing a Cleaning Schedule

Let's face it, housework is a chore. It's tiring, boring, and it never seems to end. Often you feel completely overwhelmed by the housekeeping tasks you have to face. This totally demoralizes you, so you never get going and the dirt just piles up. The good news is that once you do get started, you'll probably keep on going until it's done.

So, *how* do we get started? *Devising a cleaning schedule is the key!* Such a plan helps you to identify, organize, and prioritize individual tasks and set achievable goals. It provides an *effective time-management guide for your monthly household chores.*

To give you some idea, try taking a look at the 30-day cleaning schedule in the next chapter, which is based on one that I use daily. You can follow it as you wish, or chop 'n' change any part to tailor it to your needs.

Bear in mind, however, that the time it takes you to complete your tasks and the order in which you do them largely depends upon your skills, the amount of effort you put in, and the current state/layout of your home. Therefore, there will be aspects of my schedule (or any pre-devised schedule for that matter) that may not be fitting for your needs.

For example, because there is a lot of glass in my home, I need to spend an awful lot of time on cleaning it, probably more than you will have to. However, since my kids have moved out, I only need to deal with one bedroom on a regular basis, so I can cover everything in a single day. If you have a large family, you will have many more bedrooms to contend with, so you'll need to allocate more time for them.

The point is that the times indicated in my schedule should only be considered as rough guides and are not intended to be rigidly followed – ultimately how and when you decide to do the cleaning is up to you.

Writing a Cleaning Schedule

So how on Earth *do* you go about writing a cleaning schedule? Here are some useful tips for you to consider when devising one:

1) Find a good planner and take care of it.

You can use anything that suits you – even a printout from an electronic spreadsheet. But, make sure it won't disintegrate within a few days and is tough enough to resist spillage. You're going to be referring to it daily, and for months at a time. You'll want to keep your schedule safe, preferably in a plastic pouch or folder and look after it – it's your roadmap to a cleaner home!

2) Target the most important or dirtiest rooms first.

Cleaning can be very tiring work, so start with the most challenging tasks when you have the most energy. Moreover, you'll be making your job easier as you go along. It's far less daunting if the next task you have to face is easier to achieve than the one you've just completed.

Consider what days you are at your most energetic too. For example, if (like me) you suffer from "flaggin' Fridays" then reserve the easiest duties for that day and the hardest for the beginning of the week.

3) Break down your cleaning projects into small, manageable tasks.

As momma used to say, *"Don't try to bite off more than you can chew!"* Be realistic and don't get too ambitious! By overestimating what you can do within your allotted time, you'll either wind-up exhausted, or feel like a failure as you miss your deadlines. There's nothing more demoralizing than failure! So, take it easy on yourself and make each task as simple to achieve as possible. As a (very) general rule of thumb, try to make each task last no more than 30 minutes. Splitting your work into short, little bursts makes cleaning a lot less intimidating and more easily achievable.

4) Group related tasks together.

You can save yourself an awful lot of time and effort by grouping tasks together, i.e. wash the back door window as you wipe its frame, clean the sink as you do the toilet, etc. After all, it's a bit silly if your schedule calls for you to first vacuum the downstairs hall, next go upstairs to wash the bathroom tiles, and then back down again to dust the living room furniture. Even if that's good exercise, it'll take you twice as long to do anything.

5) Pace yourself! Spread things out a little.

While figuring out your schedule, try not to attempt to do too many back-breaking tasks on the same day. If possible, try to do the tough stuff in the first part of week, and preferably in the morning. If there are particularly arduous tasks, you can break them down even further. Remember, that once you've had a day off, you may find it difficult to get going again. Therefore, it's better to do a little bit every day of the week, rather than saving it all for one day.

6) Carefully consider the order of the tasks. Do they interfere with one another?

Consider whether a task will undo any work you've already done. For instance, always dust your furniture first before vacuuming your floor; if you do it the other way around, you'll merely be depositing dirt from your upholstery back on to your newly cleaned carpets!

7) Consider how often something needs to be done.

Some things must be cleaned more regularly than others, so make a list of the chores that need to be carried out daily, weekly, and monthly. Then consider the ones that need to be done every three to six months. For example, the laundry, dishwashing, and dusting need to be done far more frequently than shampooing the carpets (unless, you have a particularly messy pet or husband).

8) Set aside a specific time to do each task.

When you schedule time for each task, cleaning becomes integrated into your habitual, daily routine. If you begin slowly with your tasks, and build up as you do them, you'll be done before you know it!

9) Build in flexibility – prepare for the unexpected!

One golden rule in life is that even the best-laid plans go awry at some time or another – even cleaning schedules! Maybe something takes longer than you thought it would, you're having an off-day, or perhaps the washing machine decides to break down with a load of clothes still inside.

Don't panic! Just adjust your schedule to accommodate any unexpected issues you may encounter. The more flexibility you build into your daily schedule, the better chance you'll have of sticking to it. Look at your cleaning schedule as more of a roadmap rather than a set of strict rules; if one route is blocked, simply choose another to reach your goal.

One final tip is to use color-coding to make related days easier to see on a complicated schedule. For instance, if you clean the bedrooms on days 3, 9, and 14, then these entries can be in one color and the ones relating to your bathroom duties in a different color. You can even set the font for "deep-cleaning" days in bold or italics, so these entries really stand out from your lighter duty days.

All this talk of schedules and roadmaps is all very well and good, but there are times when we all feel lazy - er, I mean - *unenthusiastic*. Sometimes it's so bad that we can't even be bothered to think about cleaning the house, let alone find the effort to pick up a pencil and organize our lives properly. If you're feeling particularly unmotivated at the moment (and don't we all at times), then the next bit is for you (if it isn't too much trouble to read, of course...).

Why You're Totally Unmotivated

The good news is that you must be just a *teeny* bit motivated since you bought a book like this in the first place. So, clearly you recognize that you need to change! (Give yourself a big, sloppy kiss for making it to this first crucial step!)

There are many reasons why we may let our homes get dirty, one of which is having a negative attitude. Remember, there's a smelly, little dirt-devil in all of us! It has cunning ways of taking over by filling our brains with half-baked, excuses for doing nothing at all!

Let's take a look at some of the most common excuses:

1) I'll do it tomorrow.

I'm a sucker for this excuse myself and it's probably the number one reason why so many of our homes turn into messy sets from 1970's disaster movies.

It's because once you start putting things off, it quickly becomes a habit. The rubbish just piles up and your stuff gets dirtier and dirtier. Then, one day you realize that the quick, five-minute tidying has morphed into a ten-day deep clean!

2) I feel so overwhelmed!

If you let things get out of hand, the amount of work you have to do quickly becomes too much to face. Pretty soon, you're totally overwhelmed. As a result, nothing gets done and the situation becomes progressively worse; this leads to silly excuse number three.

3) Well, it's not that bad, is it?

After a while, we become grime-blind! We get accustomed to the piles of clothing scattered all over the furniture, that thick layer of dust on the window sill, the dingy tinge to the walls that were once painted diamond white, etc. This type of self-denial cannot only lead to a dirty home, but to esteem issues too. You will begin to lower your personal standards and lose pride in your environment. *Always be honest with yourself!*

4) I don't have the time.

This actually is *"I'll do it tomorrow!"* in disguise. It's just another type of procrastination, with a healthy dose of self-pity thrown in! It implies that you're *so* over-worked (poor thing) that you cannot even clean your home. In reality, it indicates poor time-management skills. The same result applies as before; you convince yourself that you'll *never* have the time and so nothing ever gets done.

5) It's so boring.

Few people actually like cleaning, and it's a chore that can all too easily be – and often is – avoided.

OK! OK! ENOUGH EXCUSES ALREADY! – HOW EXACTLY DO I GET MOTIVATED?

It's simple to get motivated by challenging your thoughts and using visualization techniques.

A) CHALLENGE YOUR THOUGHTS

A simple step to motivating yourself is to turn your negative thoughts upside-down, and counter them with opposing phrases. Below are a few common examples.

"I'll do it tomorrow," becomes **"I'll do it now."**

"I feel so overwhelmed," becomes **"I can do this."**

"It's not that bad," becomes **"It's HORRIBLE! I can do better than that!"**

"It's so boring," becomes ***"It's fun!"*** (Ok, this last one is a bit of a stretch, but I'll deal with it in a moment...I promise).

Try adding your own personal, negative messages and then the phrases that oppose them to this list. (REMEMBER, THERE ARE ALWAYS POSITIVE THOUGHTS TO COUNTER THE NEGATIVES – YOU JUST HAVE TO FIND THEM!)

If it helps, write down and display your thought-challenge list in a place you often look at in your home, like a notice board or the refrigerator door. Read it whenever you're troubled by negativity or the "Work of the Dirt Devil" (sounds like a 60's band).

DO IT NOW!

Often the most difficult thing to do is to get started in the first place. So, don't even think about it – just do it! The more you *think* about doing something, the more likely you are to put off doing *anything* at all.

The very act of starting something will often spur you to do even more. Think of being unmotivated as merely a wall of dominoes blocking your goal; when one falls, the others fall too.

I CAN DO THIS!

If we only focus on *how large* a challenge is, then we instantly feel overwhelmed and disheartened; there's a very simple way to combat this, however. As I said earlier, the trick is to split your cleaning challenges into manageable, bite-sized goals that you *know* you will be able to achieve with relative ease. Think of this analogy: Although, it's impossible for one man to move a heap of stone at one time, it's easy to do if he moves just a few at a time.

Remember to be patient with yourself and ALWAYS reward yourself whenever you complete a task. A bit of self-encouragement can work wonders in keeping you motivated and ready for the next challenge. However, if you are overly critical of yourself, you will only feel demoralized.

If you fail to achieve a task – DON'T BEAT YOURSELF UP! You are NOT lazy or incompetent! Failure is merely a sign that you're being overly-enthusiastic or too ambitious. We naturally over-estimate our abilities and underestimate the difficulty of things. In fact, it's something *everybody* does at one time or another. (This even happens to those who seem perfect – remember that nobody is really perfect! It's just some are more experienced or better at hiding their mistakes!)

Remember that if you fail to complete a task, try to learn from it and DON'T GIVE UP! Try, try, and try again! Slice up that problem, deal with it one bit at a time, and you WILL get there – guaranteed!

IT'S HORRIBLE! I CAN DO BETTER!

Often, we turn a blind-eye to the stuff we don't like to face (especially in the home). So, prepare to be honest with yourself, take a deep breath, and try the following exercises:

Ask yourself, what would your neighbors think if they were to walk into your home right now? What would your parents or grandparents think? What about your kids' teacher, the head of the PTA, that cop from down the road, or your local priest/preacher? Would any of them be impressed by your efforts or think you're a slob! Can you imagine any of them gossiping behind your back because of what they've just seen?

If you saw your home as a set on a TV show, what type of character would live in it? How would you feel about that character? Are you happy to identify with them or are you cringing?

Would you want to eat in a restaurant that had a kitchen in the same state as yours is now? And, what about the state of your bathroom and toilets? Would you let a stranger use them or would you feel comfortable using a bathroom that was unclean?

If you were to open a cabinet or closet in your home, what would you find? Are your belongings clean and neatly organized? Or are there piles of junk, some of which are useless and unnecessary?

One more question – has any room in your home turned into a garbage dump? Is the rest of your house generally okay, except for that one little cavern of shameful chaos? Do you barely open the door and throw stuff into the room as quickly as you can in order to avoid looking inside?

If you feel embarrassed, ashamed, or at all bad about yourself after answering these questions, then that's a good thing! It shows that you *care* what people think of you. In order to care, you *must* have some *pride* in yourself and the image you project of yourself through the environments you create. Pride is an essential motivator to get you off your behind and get scrubbing!

But, there's more to this then simply beating yourself up with the "Big Stick of Shame," – there's "The Carrot of Success and Cleanliness" to munch on too! (Sorry, I couldn't resist that phrase!)

Imagine the wonderful sense of satisfaction and pride you'll experience once you have cleaned your place up; that sense of achievement and progress as you transform each room from a cubicle of ugly chaos into a beautiful chamber of bliss!

Finally, and perhaps most importantly, just think of how much more respect you would get from others and yourself? (Phew! Pretty intoxicating stuff, isn't it?)

IT'S FUN!

"Yeah right!" you're probably thinking, but with a little creativity, cleaning can actually be fun! All you have to do is think of ways to make housework as enjoyable as possible; in other words, turn it into a game! Here are a few ideas for you to consider (try to think of even more yourself):

Play beat the clock!

One great way of making cleaning less arduous is to see how quickly you can complete a task or how many little tasks you can do within a given time.

Set the alarm on your kitchen timer or cell phone and scrub away! This can be especially useful for motivating you to do the more unpleasant household chores, like cleaning the cat's litter box or scrubbing the tiles on the kitchen ceiling. Avoid skipping over something or cutting corners; all that will do is lead to more work later on. Always make sure to do a thorough job!

Listen to music or an audio book.

Listening to music while you work is not only pleasurable, but it helps distract your attention from the sheer horror of cleaning! I listen to my iPod thingy with my earphones on and scrub away to something that has a moderate, steady beat. This is because musical beats can – quite literally – dictate the speed at which we humans work! (Industrialists have known about and used this nifty little trick for years!)

Obviously, choose something that doesn't totally grab your attention, make you work at a snail's pace, or have you running about like a demented banshee. Go for something that sits in the background for you and sets a brisk, but not exhausting, work rate.

If you only like slow waltzes or are lacking any sense of rhythm (like my husband), try listening to an audio book. You might even learn something new and useful while doing this!

Whistle while you work.

If it won't annoy the neighbors, terrify the cat, lead to incessant dog whining, shatter your wine glasses, or make you look like a complete idiot in front of everyone, try singing or whistling while you work! This advice may sound really, really stupid, but – trust me – it works wonders for keeping your spirits lifted while you're doing the stuff you dislike.

And, you don't have to just take my word for it; take a look at the role music has played in motivating and improving group morale throughout the ages. It's no coincidence that, for centuries, soldiers have been whistling, singing, playing instruments, and writing all sorts of tunes when fighting on the front lines. If whistling a happy tune can help you face the horrors of war, then surely it can help you face the horrors of a dirty oven!

Oh, and one last thing...

NEVER, EVER TURN THE TV ON! All that will do is provide a great excuse for you to sit down and watch it!

B) VISUALIZATION

Visualization is the process of imagining what you want and figuring out how to achieve it. It's a psychological mantra that has been a key concept behind dozens of self-help books for decades.

Visualization is the simple idea that by imagining success, it will come to you. However, merely *fantasizing* about a successful future won't make it happen. You will need to think about the process that needs to be completed before you can reach your goals and imagine doing those too.

There's a great spin-off exercise; by considering the *processes* that lie behind our desired *outcomes* (in our case, a clean home), we reduce our anxieties when attempting to complete those processes.

This is where a cleaning schedule is invaluable; it *forces* us to think rationally and enables us to physically *see* both our goals and the tasks that lie behind them. In turn, this reduces our sense of being overwhelmed and thus increases the likelihood of us actually *doing* something!

C) EXTRA NIFTY MOTIVATION TIPS!

This bit consists of some motivation tips you can use on top of the visualization and thought-challenging techniques discussed above. I'm sure you can think of a few more yourself!

Before you start on a particularly messy area, take a snapshot of the room you're about to work on with your cell phone or digital camera. If you find yourself slacking at any point, take a peek at the picture and it will spur you on. It will either instill shame for not getting very far or encourage you for making good progress. When you've finished cleaning the room, take another photo of it and compare it to the one you took before you began. I bet you'll be amazed at how much you've achieved! It feels good, doesn't it?

Keep the photos of the completed work and print them off. Put these prints in the same folder where you keep your schedule. These will remind you what your home *should* look like and encourage you to work on keeping it tidy in the future. It will also prove that you *can* provide a clean and organized home because you've done it before.

One great way of bringing on a sense of urgency and to get you cleaning is to throw a party!

Invite friends, family, neighbors, and anyone else you can think of to your place for a get-together. Make the invitation a week or so ahead of time (or maybe two if your home is particularly grubby). By doing this, you are setting a *real* deadline and thus giving yourself a *real* incentive not only to get cleaning, but also to do it *well*. It's amazing how effectively nosey guests are able to find any mess that you've missed!

Try setting aside a special treat for yourself for when you finish your cleaning. Make sure you use this reward *only* for cleaning and nothing else. This way you are training yourself to associate housework – quite literally – with the reward!

So, what's *my* reward? I go to the movies! I'm lucky enough to have grown-up kids, so I don't have to worry about them anymore and my hubby doesn't get home until fairly late. So, I've turned my late afternoon post-cleaning time into a lovely bit of self-indulgent "me" time! I live close to a multiplex, which also has some interesting little specialty coffee houses close by. I'll pop into the theater and watch some silly movie that I'm too embarrassed to admit I actually like. Since the place is half empty, I'm guaranteed the perfect seat at a cool price. If there's nothing showing, I'll sit in one of the cafés and watch the world go by. I ONLY do this AFTER I have finished my cleaning duties, and NEVER at any other time!

This may be hard to believe, but after doing this for a while I actually started to crave cleaning! I enjoyed my little days out so much that, in my mind, I'd "fused" my cleaning duties and started to associate them with pleasure. It works! Trust me!

Now taking a trip to the show on your own might not be your thing, but think about anything that you wouldn't normally do that you know you would like. It doesn't matter how silly or trivial it seems, do whatever floats your boat! If you start to get bored with your routine, try something else – it's that simple!

On the subject of boredom, try altering your cleaning routine occasionally and add a little variety to it. Test a different cleaning product or cleaning method to keep you from getting "stale." Obviously, avoid using a product just for the sake of it. Buy one that you think will work and won't poison the family in the process!

D) THE MOST IMPORTANT MOTIVATION TIP: – ACCEPT THAT YOU NEED TO DO IT!

This is perhaps the most important lesson you need to learn to get yourself working: accept that cleaning the home is YOUR responsibility – no one else's! Until the day nuclear-powered "tidy-bots" are invented, your house certainly won't clean itself. It's unfair to expect anyone else to do it for you (unless you're paying them).

Once you accept your fate and quit moaning about it, then you'll find cleaning a whole lot easier and less intimidating.

Therefore, it's a great idea to encourage your kids to tidy up as soon as they are able. It's easy to instill a sense of responsibility in your children while they are still very young, but it's a hell of a lot harder as they begin to reach puberty!

Moreover, if you encourage them to join you in some of the easier cleaning tasks, they may begin to associate housework with a little bit of fun. It will also teach them something about teamwork as well!

Before You Start Cleaning – Throw Your Junk Out!

One of the most effective methods of transforming any home into a cluttered, dirty mess is to hoard. Hanging on to rarely used, useless, unwanted, or outdated junk not only clutters up your home, it clutters up your life too.

Before you even dream of cleaning anything, go through your garage, as well as all the closets and cabinets in your home, and throw out anything you don't need or can live without. Donate your unwanted items or simply throw them away. It's almost impossible to clean anywhere effectively if it's filled with clutter. The very act of clearing out the clutter will make things look a thousand times better than it did without you even having to lift a duster.

The biggest problem is determining what is junk and what isn't. We can develop an unhealthy attachment to the things we own. Most of us may need a little encouragement and motivation (yes, there's *that* word again) to part with our former must-haves that we spent an awful lot of money on.

The best way to gain some useful advice about what to do with the junk you've cleared is to buy a good book on how to declutter the home. There are a few out there, but, obviously, I'm going to plug the one I wrote on the subject – so, without further ado, why not check out the following title?

The book is called, *How to Declutter Your Home for Simple Living – Decluttering Tips and Closet Organization Ideas for Creating Your Own Personal Oasis.* While I'm shamelessly promoting my work, you may be interested in the companion title for the book you're reading right now (indeed, the 30-day schedule that follows, was derived from an abbreviated schedule in the following book):

Super Simple Home Cleaning – The Best House Cleaning Tips for Green Cleaning the Home

As its title suggests, *Super Simple Home Cleaning* is packed with loads of useful tips on how to actually *do* your cleaning in the first place. It also addresses how to clean both cheaply and healthily, through the use of natural alternatives to the chemically-laden, potentially lethal products that populate our grocery store shelves.

Both of these books are available through Amazon.com.

OK, so we've covered lot of ground here on how to write an effective cleaning schedule and how to get yourself motivated to clean in the first place!

Now's your chance to put all this theory into practice! Find a pen, grab some paper, and get scheduling. In the next chapter, I've provided a sample version to help you on your way. Study it, tweak it, and make it your own. You'll be surprised on how much it will help.

Introducing – The 30-Day Cleaning Schedule

As I said earlier, you can follow this entire schedule, just bits of it, or ignore it completely if you so desire; the choice is entirely yours. It's intended primarily as a guide – not a strict timetable. It also assumes that you have already de-cluttered your home and possess some cleaning skills. For further guidance on these, check out the previously mentioned Kindle titles.

Remember that you're the one who has to actually do the cleaning; it's your responsibility – nobody else's! Now's the time to figure out what will suit you best.

One final note: in order to maintain compatibility with monochrome Kindles, I've had to remove the color-coding from the schedule provided here – sorry about that! However, I recommend you color-code your own because it'll make it *much* easier to follow.

DAY 1: QUICK CLEAN THE SURFACES AND FLOORS OF THE KITCHEN AND LIVING ROOM

First, clear away any stray items. Then, dust and clean all the surfaces in the rooms as well as sweep and/or vacuum the floors, drapes, blinds, etc.

DAY 2: QUICK CLEAN THE SURFACES AND FLOORS OF THE BATHROOM

1) Tidy it up, hang up the towels, and put any dirty ones out for washing.

2) Empty the garbage cans and replenish the toilet paper rolls.

3) Apply cleaning solution to toilets, showers, and bathtubs, leaving them there long enough to allow the spray to do its job. Next, wash away the cleaner by flushing the toilet and spraying the other fittings down with warm water. Let the cleaning solution do the work for you, but prepare to do a little light scrubbing, if necessary.

4) Wipe off and polish the mirrors, windows, counters, and cabinets.

5) Quickly, sweep/vacuum the floor, curtains, blinds, etc. Wipe down the walls and tiles if you have the time and energy.

The more you do now the less there is to do later.

6) The final task is to clear out the cabinets of empty bottles and other garbage and replenish things if needed. Make a note of anything that needs to be replaced.

DAY 3: QUICK CLEAN THE SURFACES AND FLOORS OF THE BEDROOMS

1) Pick up anything scattered on the bedroom floors (like toys, clothes, etc.) and put them back where they belong.

Remember to check under the beds, too!

2) Put any dirty clothes and bedding into your laundry hamper.

3) Working from the ceilings to the floors, clear away any dust and cobwebs from fans, light fixtures, lampshades, wall corners, windowsills, etc. Use a feather duster first (don't get a cheap one – they'll merely flail feathers everywhere), then vacuum them again using a flexible hose attachment.

4) Give any windows, pictures, and mirrors a quick spray and polish.

5) Tidy the dressers and put any items that shouldn't be on top back into the drawers. As you are tidying, throw away any junk you may find inside the drawers. (Be ruthless when deciding what to keep!)

6) Working from the top down, give the outsides of dressers and cabinets a quick dusting and cleaning.

7) When you're done, empty your waste baskets into a garbage bag.

8) Finally, make your beds. You should aim to change the bedding at least once a week.

DAY 4: QUICK CLEAN THE SURFACES AND FLOORS OF THE "EXTRA" ROOMS

By "extra rooms," I mean places like the basement, conservatory, home office, the kids' rooms, etc.

Clear away any stray items, dust and clean all the surfaces in the rooms, then briefly sweep and/or vacuum the floors, drapes, blinds, etc.

DAY 5: QUICK CLEAN THE SURFACES AND FLOORS OF THE KITCHEN AND LIVING ROOM

Repeat the same tasks as DAY 1.

DAY 6: QUICK CLEAN THE SURFACES AND FLOORS OF THE BATHROOM

Repeat the same tasks as DAY 2.

DAY 7: CLEAN ALL THE INTERIOR WINDOWS

Walk through your home and clean any mirrors and inside windows you might have missed or that need to be cleaned again. While you're doing this, clean the surfaces of counter tops, tabletops, dressers, etc. and continue to tidy up.

One little tip to clean your mirrors without leaving streaks is to wipe them over with old newspapers, dampened with a drop of white vinegar.

DAY 8: SWEEP AND VACUUM ALL THE FLOORS AND STAIRS (OPTIONAL: DEEP CLEANING)

As the subtitle cunningly suggests, walk through your home, and sweep and vacuum all the carpets and rugs you have. Sweep and then use the hose-attachment to vacuum all the stairs. Make sure you get into all the little nooks and crannies. Remember that someone's bare feet may end up on those floors, so make sure you do a thorough job.

Now you have three choices:

1. Put your feet up and have a nice cup of coffee.

2. Sweep and vacuum any other "extra room" in the house.

3. Deep clean the carpets – focusing mainly on the stairs (i.e. wash them in carpet cleaner or steam clean).

I think I can guess which one you'll *want* to choose. But remember that what you put off today, you'll only need to do later. So, the job will get progressively worse over time! Sorry to nag, but you know it makes sense!

DAY 9: QUICK CLEAN THE SURFACES AND FLOORS OF THE BEDROOMS

Repeat the same tasks as DAY 3.

DAY 10: DEEP CLEAN THE LIVING ROOM

The goals here are to thoroughly clean and organize the living room, so it will only need a quick dust and wipe-over the rest of the week. As with any deep cleaning, it may take a bit longer to do than expected, so don't be afraid to spread the work over to the following day if necessary. Just make sure you complete all the duties outlined for that day.

1) Pick up stray items and lift up the rugs

Pick up any items that are out of place and put them back where they belong. If you have area rugs, lift them up and place them in another room.

2) Clear racks and desks

Empty out-of-date stuff from your magazine racks. Clear your desk of any clutter or junk mail that might have piled up.

3) Lights and fixtures

Dust all the fans, light fixtures, lampshades, and accessible parts of the walls. Take down the fixtures and wash them, if necessary. Put them back up only AFTER the ceiling is dry if you intend to wash it later.

4) Ceiling

Dust away cobwebs from the ceiling and get rid of any other "nasties" you may find. Pay particular attention to the corners. If you're feeling brave, wash the ceiling, too. If you've had to take things down at this point, don't put them back up until the ceiling is dry.

5) Wash windows and frames

Thoroughly spray and polish both sides of the window panes, frames, sills, and any pictures or mirrors you might have. Don't forget the tops of them, too!

6) Vacuum and de-clutter wall units, shelves, and display cabinets

Carefully empty any little trinkets from these into a cardboard box. Try to place them in some order, so that at the end you can figure out where everything belongs on the shelves and in the cabinets.

Carefully spray and dust these items as you lay them out. Pay special attention to your media collections and books – these are real dust-traps!

Working from the top down, give the insides of your units, drawers, and shelves a thorough dusting, vacuuming, and cleaning.

Once you've finished, return everything to where it was and throw out anything you don't really need – a cluttered home is an untidy home!

7) Empty and wash your wastebaskets

Your wastebaskets are probably full now, so empty them, clean them, and replace their liners.

8) Pull your furniture out to the center of the room and clean the floor underneath them

Pull *all* your furniture into the center of the room, and sweep and vacuum the patches of the floor they once stood on, plus a few extra inches around them. Wash or mop any area as needed. Factor in the time it will take for these patches to dry because it's a bad idea to move your furniture back onto a damp carpet or floor.

9) Wash the parameter of the floor and the hard-to-reach places

Now that you've pulled out all the furniture, it's the time to tackle those hard-to-reach places. Wash baseboards, doors, and doorframes (don't forget the tops). Wipe off the wall sockets with an almost dry cloth.

Next, sweep and vacuum about 18 inches around the perimeter of the floor. Wash or mop any area that needs it. Factor in the time it will take for these patches to dry (for the reason mentioned earlier)!

10) Clean your furniture and then move it back to where it belongs

Give the upholstery of your soft furnishings a good cleaning. You might even want to hit the cushions a few times to lift the dust. Then, thoroughly vacuum all of your furniture. Try to get rid of any marks or stains, too. Also, vacuum the inside lining of the couch/chairs and the frames. If you can't disassemble them, be sure to check down the sides of your chairs and the back of the couch; you never know – you might find a small fortune in loose change lurking there!

If you have the time, polish your furniture, too.

11) Move back your furniture

Once you're done and the floor is bone dry, move your furniture back into place. As I said before, never move furniture back onto a wet floor (unless you want to encourage mold growth).

12) Re-dust everything

Cleaning the furniture is a dirty job, so it's inevitable that you'll need to dust it off again. Don't forget the TV screens and hi-fi units because they seem to just love to suck up the dust.

13) Clean the rest of the floor

You should have already dealt with the edge of the floor and under the furniture, so it's time to properly clean the center of the floor. Sweep, vacuum, and then wash or steam-clean it if necessary. Run a mop over the floor if you don't have a carpet.

14) Clean and return the rugs

Finally (phew!), beat, sweep, vacuum, or clean your area rugs and put them back where they were. You're done! Now, you can kick back and have that cup of coffee!

DAY 11: QUICK CLEAN THE SURFACES AND FLOORS OF THE BATHROOM

Repeat the same tasks as DAY 2.

DAY 12: CLEAN OUT THE CLOSETS

The goal here is to empty your closets of the stuff you don't need and organize your clothing. Hopefully, this will eliminate the problems of constantly running out of storage or endlessly rummaging through the closet looking for something to wear.

The first step is to empty everything (and I do mean *everything*) out of your closet, and carefully place it on the bed. Keep the clothes on their hangers and lay them out as flat as possible.

Next, working from the top down, give the insides of the closet, including its shelves and any drawers it might have, a thorough spray 'n' wipe and vacuuming. Don't forget those corners!

When you're done, weed out the junk! Sort the clothes into three piles: one for keeping, one for donating, and one for trashing!

Carefully, place the donation pile into a suitably sturdy container and throw the trash into garbage bags for disposal and/or recycling.

Now, go through the clothes you are keeping, consider which ones you're likely to wear this season, and pack away any that won't be worn until the next one. Put the ones for next season to one side, so they can be vacuum-sealed (preferably) and boxed away somewhere nice and dry.

Next, give the "in-season" clothes a good 'ole sniff! Do any of them smell a little funky? If they do, put them aside for washing. Don't make your glamorous attire into a stinky pile of rags and then return it back to your closet without washing it.

Then, take your clean, in-season clothing and start grouping similar items together (like your mittens and gloves together, hats together, jackets together, etc.), and hang each group back up (or place in drawers or shelves – whatever is appropriate) in order of size. Voila! You've organized your closet and probably found some extra space to boot!

Finally, close the doors and, working from the top down, give the outsides of the closet a good 'ole spray and polish!

DAY 13: QUICK CLEAN THE SURFACES AND FLOORS OF THE "EXTRA" ROOMS

Same deal as DAY 4, but with one proviso: If you feel any of these rooms would benefit from a deep clean, then go for it! Why not deep clean all of them, if you're feeling particularly heroic?

DAY 14: DEEP CLEAN THE BEDROOMS

The goals here are to thoroughly clean the bedroom and organize it. Then, it'll only need a quick dusting and wipe-down the rest of the week. The duties are very similar to those of the quick clean, but with a few added goodies thrown in! As with all deep cleaning, it may take a bit longer to do than expected. So, don't be afraid to spread the work over to the following day if necessary – just make sure you complete all the duties outlined for that day.

1) Pick up stuff and gather the laundry

As you did with the quick clean, pick up any items that are scattered on the floors and under the beds and neatly put them back where they belong.

Put any dirty clothes and bedding into your laundry hamper.

2) Lights and fixtures

Dust the fans, light fixtures, lampshades, and the accessible parts of the walls. Take down the fixtures for washing, if necessary. Put them back AFTER the ceiling is dry, if you intend to wash it later.

3) Ceiling

Dust the ceiling, removing cobwebs and any other "nasties" you may find. Pay particular attention to the corners. If you're feeling brave, wash the ceiling, too. If you've had to take anything down at this point, put it back up, once the ceiling is dry.

4) Wash windows and frames

Thoroughly spray and polish both sides of the window panes and their frames, as well as any pictures or mirrors you might have.

5) Polish the furniture

Thoroughly dust and polish any chairs and other bits of furniture you have in your bedroom.

6) Clean the drawers of your dresser

Deal with each drawer, one at a time.

Empty the contents of the drawer into a tray, cardboard box, or any appropriate container, so you can keep your stuff together without losing anything.

Give the insides of the empty drawer a thorough spray 'n' wipe and dusting, making sure you get into all the corners.

Return your jewelry, makeup, etc. once you have finished. As you put everything away, examine each item. Ask yourself if you really need an item and be ruthless about throwing things away. Now is the chance for you to begin de-cluttering your bedroom!

7) Removing your bed linens

Now the most important job – changing your bed linens: Pull off all the bedding, pillowcases, duvet, and duvet covers, and throw them into the hamper (check their labels before you actually wash them though).

Now vacuum your mattress and as much of the bedframe as you can with the hose attachment. Try to remove as much dust up as possible!

Next, flip your mattress and vacuum the other side, if you can. If it's too heavy for you to turn yourself, get someone to help you. Turning a mattress not only spreads wear and tear, it also helps prevent the buildup of mold and other "nasties," like pollen, dust mites, etc. (Don't go there!). You may need to vacuum the bedframe again to pick up any particles that have fallen while turning the mattress.

8) Clean the floor

Now, it's time to *properly* deal with the floor. Completely clear the floor of all area rugs, bins, etc. and place them somewhere out of the room. Depending of what type of floor you have, sweep or thoroughly vacuum under the bed and any furniture that you can move, like chairs, tables, etc. Then, clean the rest of the floor. Run a mop over it if you don't have a carpeted bedroom.

9) Make the bed, using fresh bedding

Now it's time to put back any area rugs and moved furniture. Finally, remake your bed with fresh, clean bedding, pillowcases, duvets etc.

DAY 15: QUICK CLEAN THE SURFACES AND FLOORS OF THE KITCHEN AND LIVING ROOM

Repeat the same tasks as DAY 1.

DAY 16: DEEP CLEAN THE BATHROOMS

The idea here is to get your bathroom really clean and sparkling, so it'll only need a quick bit of maintenance the rest of the week. This may take a while, so don't be surprised if you go over your scheduled slot. Don't panic! You can always find the extra time by spreading it over into tomorrow's quick cleaning duties.

1) Pick up stuff and put it in the laundry

As before with the quick clean, pick up any items that are scattered on the floors and put them back where they belong.

Put any dirty towels into your laundry hamper.

2) Lights and fixtures

Dust fans, light fixtures, and the assessable parts of the walls. Take down the fixtures for washing if necessary. Put them back AFTER the ceiling has been cleaned.

3) Ceiling

Dust away the cobwebs or any other "nasties" you may find from the ceiling, paying particular attention to the corners. If you're feeling brave, wash the ceiling too. If you've had to take anything down at this point, put it back up when the ceiling is completely dry.

4) Inside the toilet

Thoroughly scrub the inside of the toilet bowl, making sure to get under the rims. Then, flush and squirt in some toilet cleaner. Leave it soaking while you get on with the other cleaning in your bathroom.

Go back after letting the cleaner soak in the toilet. Scrub and flush again. You might even want to drizzle some bleach around the inside of the bowl up into the rim.

5) Garbage cans

Give the inside and outside of your garbage cans a thorough cleaning, and then apply a mild disinfectant. Don't skip this last step because garbage is a breeding ground for germs!

6) Bathroom cabinets and under-sink units

Wash them from the top to the floor. If you find any items that shouldn't be on the top of the units, put things back where they belong or get rid of them if they are unnecessary. (Be ruthless about what to leave behind!)

Empty the units and give both the inside and outside a good spray and scrub. Deal with them, one shelf at a time, and put the emptied items into a cardboard box to keep them together.

7) Countertops

Take a long, hard look at them! Try to keep your countertops as clean and clutter-free as possible. Throw away any stuff you don't need and store as much you can underneath, not on top of the counter.

Thoroughly spray down your counters and methodically scrub away every little spot of lime-scale, toothpaste-speckle, soap-scum, and mold you find. The more you remove here, the less work you'll need to do the rest of the week. Wipe off the particularly damp and moldy areas with a mild disinfectant to prevent bacterial or fungal growth.

8) Mirrors, tiles, windows, and walls

Give your bathroom tiles and glass a thorough wash and polish. Pay particular attention to the tops of mirrors hanging on the wall. If necessary, take them off the wall as you dust them. Give any grout lines a good scrubbing with an appropriate cleaner and an old toothbrush.

9) Curtains and blinds

Vacuum any blinds, if you have them and/or change the curtains.

10) Sink basin and faucets

Spray the whole unit over with an all-purpose cleaner and let it soak for a while. Next, thoroughly scrub the faucets, drain-hole, and even the plug – this can get very yucky after a while. Then, scrub the basin, both inside and out. Make sure you clean up as much dirt as you can, and then give everything a final rinse over in warm water to remove the cleaning solution.

11) Outside the toilet

Thoroughly wipe-clean the outside of the toilet (including the cistern and seat) with a mild disinfectant cleaner.

12) Floor

Start by sweeping or vacuuming the floor. Make sure you don't neglect the corners! Next, wash the baseboards. Finally, give the floor a thorough mopping with an all-purpose soap and a mild disinfectant.

DAY 17: CLEAN YOUR ELECTRONICS AND THE REGULARLY-TOUCHED PARTS OF THE HOUSE

Walk through your home and polish and dust anything with an electrical plug on it (including the plugs and cables themselves) – and I do mean *everything;* from your humble desk lamps, to your toaster, blender, etc. Don't forget your massive 70" LED TV that cost you a fortune.

Make sure you only use a cleaner that's appropriate for the job, as some electronics have special plastic or metal finishes with erasable labeling. Remember to unplug an item before you spray it if you want to avoid getting shocked or electrocuted. While items are unplugged, sort and organize any tangled cords and cables so you can see, at a glance, what is connected to where.

While walking through, clean any items that are regularly touched, such as doorknobs, phones, remote controls, switches, switch plates, banisters, etc.

DAY 18: CLEAN OUT THE REFRIGERATOR, TAKE STOCK OF FOOD, AND ORGANIZE THE PANTRY

Empty your fridge and place the food in the sink, packed with bags of ice. Throw out anything that is spoiled or out of date. Next, wash every inch of the fridge, inside and out – including the shelves, salad drawer, door, door seals, and frame – and make sure you clean the inside corners of the fridge, too.

When it's time to put stuff back in, organize your fridge by the recommended temperature for each item, so food stays fresher for longer.

Heat rises, so the coldest part is in the back on the bottom; dairy products and freshly squeezed juices should go there.

Place packaged meat and cold cuts on the coldest, bottom shelf, with fruit and veggies on the shelves immediately above.

The center of the fridge provides the most consistent temperature, so place your eggs on the middle shelf.

Use the door or upper shelves for butter, condiments, pasteurized juices, and sodas.

When organizing the pantry, empty the shelves, and get rid of anything that's about to expire. Scrub and dust the inside and shelves of the pantry. When you're done, return your items, placing the oldest perishables at the front (i.e. the foods closest to their expiration dates) with the newest / least perishable at the back.

DAY 19: CLEAN ENTRANCEWAYS, SWEEP THE PORCH, AND CLEAN OUT THE CAR (OPTIONAL: GARAGE)

Return anything that's in your entranceways and porches, but shouldn't be, back to where it belongs. Then, dust, vacuum, or sweep where appropriate. Start with the ceiling and work your way to the floor, paying special attention to the corners. Wash or mop the floor, if required. Don't forget to clean the light fixtures, too!

Now it's time to clean out the car! Treat it the same as any other room; remove *everything*, trash the junk, remove the seats (if possible), vacuum and wipe clean the interior, vacuum the seats, put back in what you need (don't forget the seats), and then wash the exterior. (OK. I'll let you off easy with a visit to the carwash here).

Do you have a garage? Now's the time to tackle it! The first job is to dust and eliminate any cobwebs that may be lurking in the corners. Next, is the primary job – de-cluttering the garage! Go through your stuff and throw out any junk you find, dusting the shelves as you go. A good sweep of the floor is essential! Get that garage organized!

DAY 20: QUICK CLEAN THE SURFACES AND FLOORS OF THE KITCHEN AND LIVING ROOM

Repeat the same tasks as DAY 1.

DAY 21: QUICK CLEAN THE SURFACES AND FLOORS OF THE BATHROOM

Repeat the same tasks as DAY 2.

DAY 22: QUICK CLEAN THE SURFACES AND FLOORS OF THE BEDROOMS

Repeat the same tasks as DAY 3.

DAY 23: SWEEP AND VACUUM ALL THE FLOORS AND STAIRS (OPTIONAL: DEEP CLEAN)

Repeat the same tasks as DAY 8.

DAY 24: CLEAN AND ORGANIZE THE LINEN CLOSET

Pull out all your towels, sheets, pillowcases, etc. and place them on a clean, flat surface. Weed out anything which may need to be washed; if there's linen that hasn't been used for a while, it may go a little musty.

Next, organize everything by grouping similar items together, (pillowcases with pillowcases, bed sheets with bed sheets, towels with towels, etc.). It's a great idea to keep sets of bedding together by filling your duvet covers with their matching linens. Put matching pillowcases inside one another, too. Try to keep everything as flat as possible.

Now, dust and then vacuum the inside of the closet, using the hose attachment. Work from the top down, starting with the corners.

When you're done, return your groups of linens and towels to the closet. Think about what is used least and place that stuff toward the back or top. Put the most used items (like towels) at the front.

Finally give the outside of the closet a thorough dusting and wipe down (as usual work from the top down).

DAY 25: QUICK CLEAN THE SURFACES AND FLOORS OF THE KITCHEN AND LIVING ROOM

This is your final quick clean of the month. Repeat the same process as DAY 1. This will also serve to prepare you for tomorrow's deep cleaning, and will give you a clearer idea of what still needs to be done.

DAY 26: DEEP CLEAN THE KITCHEN

The goals here are to thoroughly clean and organize the kitchen, so it will only need a quick dust and wipe down the rest of the week. This may take a while, so don't be surprised if you go over your scheduled slot. No need to worry though because you can always find the extra time by spilling over into tomorrow's quick cleaning duties.

1) Light fixtures

The first job is to wash, vacuum, or spray the light fixtures. If necessary, soak the fixtures in the sink. Don't put them back up just yet, because we need to clean the ceiling first. (But, when the time comes, make sure they are thoroughly dry before you put them back up.)

2) Ceiling

Next, dust the ceiling to get rid of cobwebs or any other "nasties" you may find, paying particular attention to the corners. Then, wash the ceiling. If you've had to take them down, put back up your fixtures once the ceiling is dry.

3) Curtains and blinds

Vacuum any blinds, if you have them and/or change the curtains.

4) Cabinets and shelving

Start at the top and work your way to the floor. If you find any stuff that shouldn't be there, put the things back where they belong or trash the junk. (Be ruthless here when deciding what to keep!)

Begin by emptying the cabinets/shelves of their contents and placing the emptied items into a cardboard box temporarily. Focus on one cabinet and do one shelf at a time and then move on to the next, repeating the process. Give the insides a good spray and scrub. Remember the corners! Don't worry about polishing the silverware just yet – we'll deal with that at another time!

You're done? Cool! Put all that stuff away and move on!

5) Countertops

Take a long, hard look at your counters! Try to keep your countertops as clean and clutter-free as possible. Throw away any stuff you don't need, and store as much as you can underneath the counters, not on top of them.

Thoroughly spray down your countertops and take your time removing every little spot and grease mark. The more you remove here, the less work you will need to do moving forward.

6) The stove

Now, the fun really begins! Spray the top of your stove and make sure its burners are thoroughly clean. If you have metal burners, leave them soaking in cleaning solution in your sink. This will help soften away the burnt-on grease as you get on with the rest of your cleaning.

Next, thoroughly clean the inside and outside of the oven and its door. Take your time and make sure you put some newspaper in front of the oven door in case any yucky half-melted gunk spills out onto the floor.

Then, wash the wall directly behind the stove. If it's starting to look a little funky, then scrub and clean. Retrieve the metal burners from the sink, dry them off, and put them back on the stovetop.

7) Other appliances and garbage cans

Scrub and clean other appliances, such as the dishwasher, washing machine, and microwave. Wipe down the outside of the refrigerator again. A good tip for cleaning the inside of a microwave is to place a bowl of water with a drop of lemon juice in it and zap the bowl at full power for about 5-10 minutes. The lemony steam that's produced will melt off the gunk from the walls of the microwave with no effort from you at all! Don't forget to wash out the trash cans too, both inside *and* out! Always apply a mild disinfectant to the cans to kill any nasty bugs and germs lurking in them.

8) Walls, windows, and tiles

Give the rest of the kitchen walls, the windows, and the tiles a good wash and wipe down. Scrub any grout lines with an appropriate cleaner and an old toothbrush.

9) Sink basin and faucets

Spray the whole unit over with an all-purpose cleaner and let it soak for a while. Next, thoroughly scrub and clean the faucets, drain-hole, and even the plug – this can get pretty yucky after a while. Then, scrub the basin, both inside and out. Make sure you bring up as much dirt as you can, and then give everything a final rinse over in warm water to remove the cleaning solution.

10) Floor

Start by sweeping or vacuuming the floor. Make sure you don't neglect the corners! Next, wash the baseboards. Finally, give the floor a thorough mopping with an all-purpose soap and a mild disinfectant.

DAY 27: QUICK CLEAN THE SURFACES AND FLOORS OF THE BATHROOM

Do your final quick clean of the bathroom for the month, the same as DAY 2.

DAY 28: QUICK CLEAN THE SURFACES AND FLOORS OF THE BEDROOMS

Do your final quick clean of the bedroom for the month, the same as DAY 3.

DAY 29: CLEAN ONE THING YOU HAVEN'T HAD THE CHANCE TO CLEAN YET

It's easy to fall behind with your schedule; things may take longer than they should or you could have been diverted by an unexpected event or emergency.

Therefore, use today as a "catch-up" day; if you haven't done so already, deep clean your stove, wipe down all the light fixtures, or tackle that particularly difficult job you've been putting off all week! (Naughty you!)

DAY 30: Sweep and vacuum all the floors and stairs (Optional: Deep clean)

Do your final quick sweep/vacuum of the month, the same as DAY 8.

Conclusion

Now, that you've reached the end of this book, let's briefly review what we've covered. We've discussed why doing your own housework is a good idea, why we can't be bothered to do it in the first place, and how to combat our apathy through visualization. Finally, I've provided you with a sample cleaning plan for you to build upon (with a few organizational and cleaning tips thrown in for good measure).

Hopefully, you're now in the process of devising your own, customized cleaning schedule, and you're ready to face the horror of housework! Then, maybe – ever so slowly – you'll begin to enjoy it. Housework *can* be fun - *honest!*

About the Author

Judith Turnbridge is a married artist with an interest in interior design. She enjoys painting, calligraphy, and caring for her garden. Her two children have now grown up and flown the nest, and the two hungry mouths she now feeds belong to her two fluffy cats.

Other books by Judith Turnbridge:

Super Simple Home Cleaning: The Best House Cleaning Tips for Green Cleaning the Home

How to Organize Your Life to Maximize Your Day: Effective Time Management Tips and Ideas to Simplify Your Life

How to Declutter Your Home for Simple Living: Decluttering Tips and Closet Organization Ideas for Creating Your Own Personal Oasis

Out of Sight, Out of Mind: Easy Home Organization Tips and Storage Solutions for Clutter-Free Living

Nature's Miracle Elixir: The Essential Health Benefits of Coconut Oil

How to Survive a Disaster: Emergency Preparedness for You and Your Family

23236217R00030

Printed in Great Britain
by Amazon